BUGS & CRITTERS

Written by:	**Brian Holley** Supervisor, Children's Garden Royal Botanical Gardens
Editors:	**Nadia Pelowich** **Paul Hayes** **Curtis Rush**
Design:	**J.T. Winik**
Illustration:	**Diane Gruettner, Diane Black** **Denis Gagne**
Cover Art:	**Rick Rowden**

ISBN 0-87617-020-3

Penworthy
PUBLISHING COMPANY

219 North Milwaukee Street, Milwaukee, Wisconsin 53202

Printed in Hong Kong

Watch for the bugs with the amazing insect trivia!

INSECTS are different from animals!

ALL INSECTS HAVE: six legs, a tough covering on the outside of their bodies called an exoskeleton, and three body parts — the head, thorax and abdomen.

Each body segment of an insect has a separate role:

The head (like ours) contains a mouth, eyes and a brain, but the insect also has antennae, which are very sensitive to nearby movement.

The abdomen contains the heart, digestive and breathing organs.

STOCKY LESTES

HEAD ▼

BUMBLEBEE

LUNA MOTH

THORAX ▲

ABDOMEN ▲

The thorax is the locomotion center. It is full of large muscles that move the wings and legs.

LADY BEETLE

CENTIPEDE

INSECTS DON'T HAVE:

Bones — Mammals, fish, birds, amphibians and reptiles have internal skeletons made up of bones.

Noses — Insects usually smell with their antennae. Some butterflies and moths even smell with their feet!

WHICH OF THESE ARE INSECTS?

Some of these creatures are not insects; they are called noninsects.

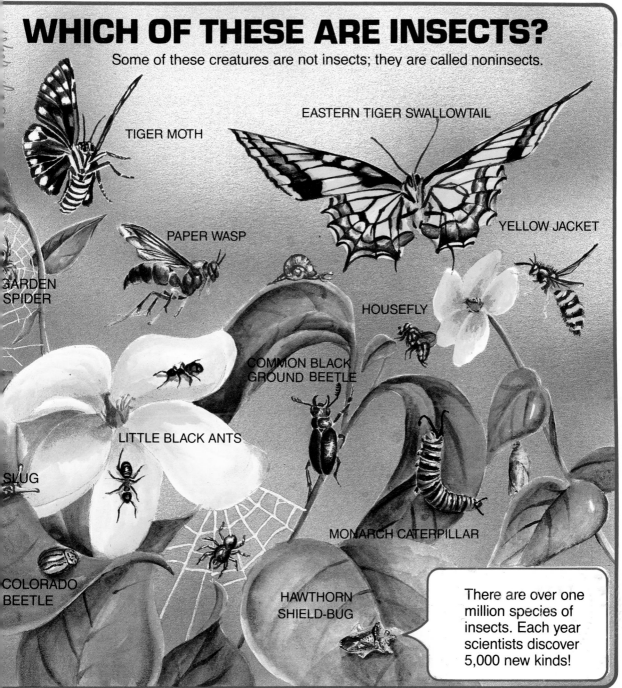

TIGER MOTH

EASTERN TIGER SWALLOWTAIL

YELLOW JACKET

PAPER WASP

GARDEN SPIDER

HOUSEFLY

COMMON BLACK GROUND BEETLE

LITTLE BLACK ANTS

SLUG

MONARCH CATERPILLAR

COLORADO BEETLE

HAWTHORN SHIELD-BUG

There are over one million species of insects. Each year scientists discover 5,000 new kinds!

THE SKINNY WAISTS AND THE SCALY WINGS

Scientists look for common features when they group insects. Many insects can be divided into two groups: insects with skinny waists and insects with scaly wings.

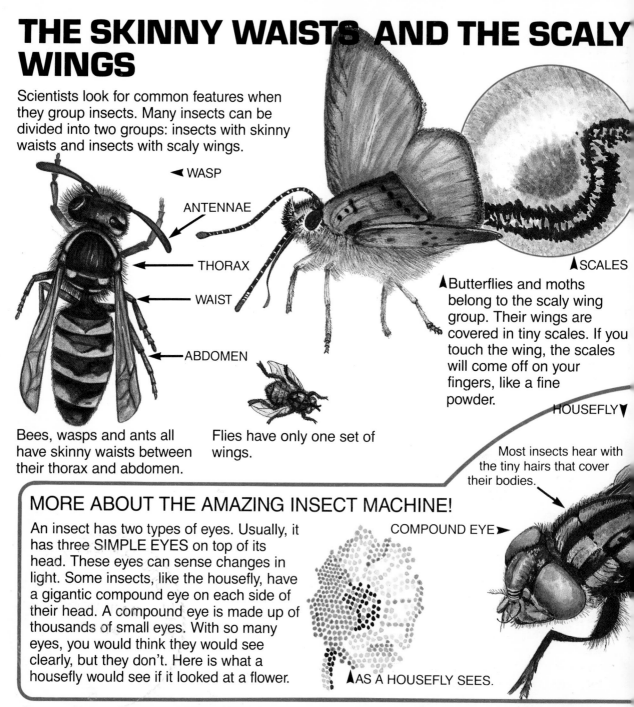

◄ WASP

ANTENNAE

THORAX

WAIST

ABDOMEN

▲SCALES

▲Butterflies and moths belong to the scaly wing group. Their wings are covered in tiny scales. If you touch the wing, the scales will come off on your fingers, like a fine powder.

HOUSEFLY▼

Bees, wasps and ants all have skinny waists between their thorax and abdomen.

Flies have only one set of wings.

Most insects hear with the tiny hairs that cover their bodies.

MORE ABOUT THE AMAZING INSECT MACHINE!

An insect has two types of eyes. Usually, it has three SIMPLE EYES on top of its head. These eyes can sense changes in light. Some insects, like the housefly, have a gigantic compound eye on each side of their head. A compound eye is made up of thousands of small eyes. With so many eyes, you would think they would see clearly, but they don't. Here is what a housefly would see if it looked at a flower.

COMPOUND EYE➤

▲AS A HOUSEFLY SEES.

4

Beetles have hard coverings, which protect their wings. These hard wings look like part of the beetle's back. They lift up when the beetle prepares to take off.▼

The wings of birds are strengthened with bones, but an insect's wings have a net of thin, hard tubes to support them.

TUBES

THESE ANIMALS HAVE EXOSKELETONS LIKE INSECTS BUT . . .

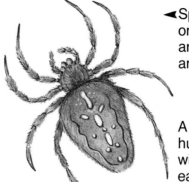

◄Spiders have eight legs and only two body parts. They are not insects, but arachnids.

A millipede has up to one hundred body segments, with two pairs of legs on each.▼

This makes it a myriapod, not an insect.

INSECTS ARE INCREDIBLY STRONG.

An ant can carry 450 times ➤ its own weight! If you could do the same, you could carry a bus! If an ant were as big as you, though, its exoskeleton would be so heavy that it wouldn't be able to move its own body around.

A flea can jump 200 times the length of its body! Olympic long jumpers can jump only three times the length of their bodies.

ACTUAL SIZE OF A FLEA •

CHANGING ARMOR

The hard covering (exoskeleton) on an insect's body is like a suit of armor. It can't grow. Insects keep a new set of armor folded up inside their bodies. When an insect grows too big for its armor, the armor splits. A new skin then unfolds and hardens into a new exoskeleton. Insects change armor several times before they become adults.

Tent caterpillar eggs form a crystalline ring on a branch.

Lacewing eggs are supported by slender strands.

Ladybird beetles lay up to 1,000 tiny capsules on leaves.

INCOMPLETE METAMORPHOSIS.

Some young insects look like miniature adult insects. They just have to grow bigger. These insects have three stages of development instead of four:

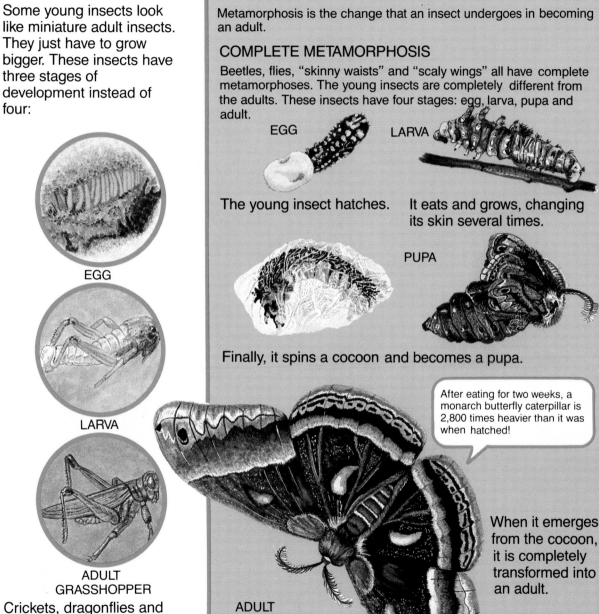

EGG

LARVA

ADULT
GRASSHOPPER

Crickets, dragonflies and cicadas also have incomplete metamorphoses.

PRESTO! METAMORPHOSIS!

Metamorphosis is the change that an insect undergoes in becoming an adult.

COMPLETE METAMORPHOSIS

Beetles, flies, "skinny waists" and "scaly wings" all have complete metamorphoses. The young insects are completely different from the adults. These insects have four stages: egg, larva, pupa and adult.

EGG

LARVA

The young insect hatches.

It eats and grows, changing its skin several times.

PUPA

Finally, it spins a cocoon and becomes a pupa.

After eating for two weeks, a monarch butterfly caterpillar is 2,800 times heavier than it was when hatched!

When it emerges from the cocoon, it is completely transformed into an adult.

ADULT

WASPS

Wasps provide a great variety of nurseries for their young.

A potter wasp makes a clay nest. After laying an egg inside, she captures caterpillars and puts them into the nest. The opening is then plugged. When the egg hatches, the larva will feed on the caterpillars. ➤

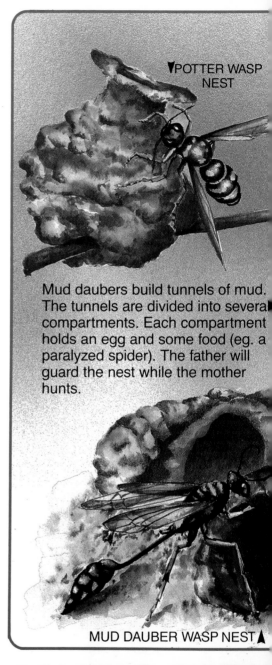

▼POTTER WASP NEST

Mud daubers build tunnels of mud. The tunnels are divided into several compartments. Each compartment holds an egg and some food (eg. a paralyzed spider). The father will guard the nest while the mother hunts.

MUD DAUBER WASP NEST▲

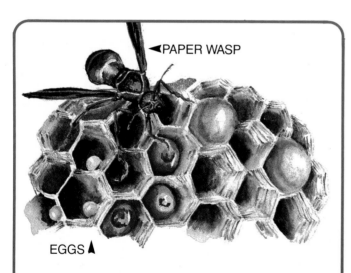

◄PAPER WASP

EGGS▲

A paper wasp chews wood into a pulp and spreads it in thin layers to make its nest. Each cell is perfectly formed into a five-sided pentagonal shape.

TAKING CARE

NATURE'S OWN WAY . . .

◄Some wasps lay their eggs in the bodies of caterpillars. When the eggs hatch into larvae, they will eat the caterpillar. But they must watch out! There are wasps that lay their eggs in the larvae of other wasps!

▼MOSSY ROSE GALL WASP

The mossy rose gall wasp lays its eggs in the stems of rose bushes. The sting of the wasp triggers abnormal growth in the plant. The young insects are well-protected inside this strange nest.

TRIVIA
Many animals are afraid of the wasp's sting. Some insects, like the flowerfly, mimic the coloring of the wasp to fool predators.

▲NOTE: These nests are usually built horizontally on steep banks or walls of buildings.

OF BABY ▪ ▪ ▪ ▪

INSECT CITIES

Some insects, like termites, live in large groups. The cities they build are amazing!

A type of African termite builds insect skyscrapers, 6 m (20 ft.) across!

SOLDIER
TERMITE

Termites in North America are more likely to be found in wood. Unfortunately, the wood in which they make their homes could be part of your house.

Honey is the reserve food of the hive. It is made by evaporating water from the nectar. Bees will sometimes beat their wings to create a breeze which "dries" the nectar. This speeds up the honey-making process. ►

2 When the worker is ▲ three weeks old, it leaves the hive to collect pollen and nectar. A worker has baskets on its rear legs to carry pollen.

LIFE IN THE HIVE

Bees also live in large groups. Their cities, like ours, are buzzing with activity. There are many jobs to be done. Let's look at the honeybee's hive.

3 The worker develops special glands which produce wax. For the next week, it builds and repairs the combs with the wax.➤

◄ The hive is divided into combs. Each comb is made up of many small six-sided cells. These are used for storing honey or pollen and as nurseries for bee larvae.

A worker bee tells others about the location of nectar by doing a special dance. The speed and pattern of this dance indicates the direction, distance and quantity of the nectar.

When the hive becomes overcrowded, the old queen and part of the colony will look for a new home.➤

Each hive contains one queen. She spends her life laying eggs.

◄Honeybee hives have about 60,000 worker bees. For the first two weeks, a worker cares for and feeds the larvae. Follow the worker bee's life to stage numbers 2 and 3.

The drone is a male bee.▲ His only job is to mate with a new queen. There are about 1,000 drones in a hive.

TRIVIA
Honeybees are the only domesticated insect in North America! They were brought here by settlers in the 17th century.

ANTS
RAIDERS, FARMERS AND RANCHERS

Most ants live underground, but a few build hills. Some anthills are a meter (3 ft.) or more in diameter!

When a ringleader ant starts working, others follow to help. How do the ringleaders know what has to be done? No one knows. It's a mystery!

> **TRIVIA**
> Queen ants may live up to 15 years!

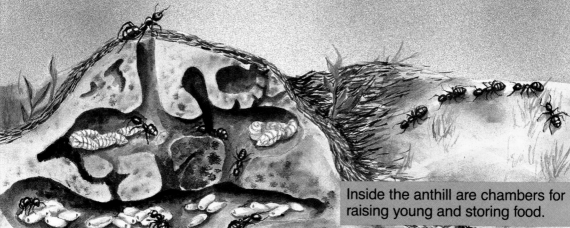

Inside the anthill are chambers for raising young and storing food.

Ants have poor vision, but they have an excellent sense of smell. When an ant finds food, it marks the trail with a scent for the other workers to follow. Try testing this. When you see a line of ants, try rubbing your finger across their path. What happens?

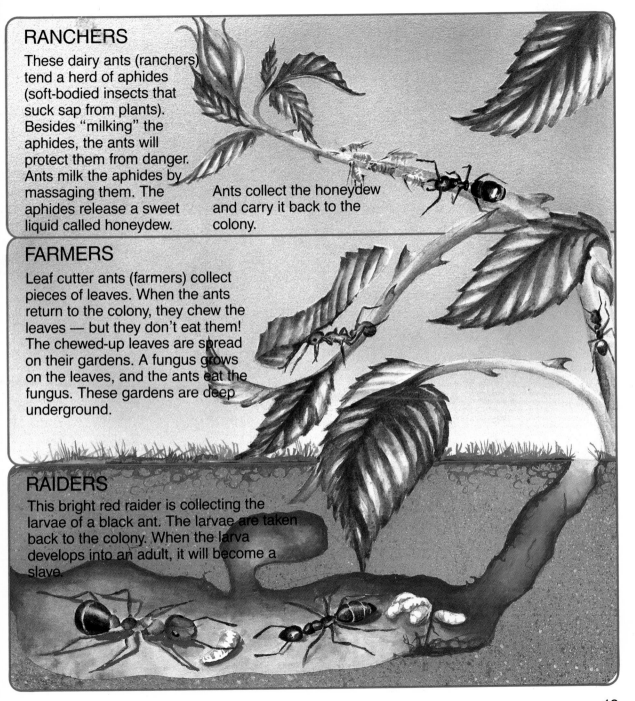

RANCHERS

These dairy ants (ranchers) tend a herd of aphides (soft-bodied insects that suck sap from plants). Besides "milking" the aphides, the ants will protect them from danger. Ants milk the aphides by massaging them. The aphides release a sweet liquid called honeydew.

Ants collect the honeydew and carry it back to the colony.

FARMERS

Leaf cutter ants (farmers) collect pieces of leaves. When the ants return to the colony, they chew the leaves — but they don't eat them! The chewed-up leaves are spread on their gardens. A fungus grows on the leaves, and the ants eat the fungus. These gardens are deep underground.

RAIDERS

This bright red raider is collecting the larvae of a black ant. The larvae are taken back to the colony. When the larva develops into an adult, it will become a slave.

13

CREATURES AROUND THE HOUSE

These creatures like to share your home. Some of them are insects and some are noninsects. Each has a special room or area of your house it prefers.

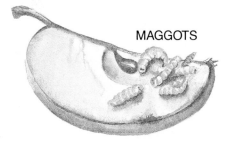

MAGGOTS

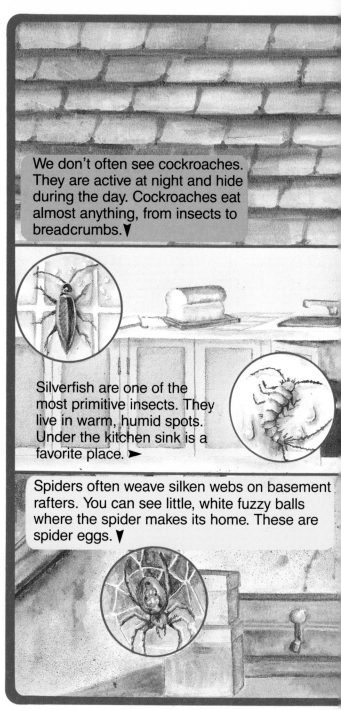

We don't often see cockroaches. They are active at night and hide during the day. Cockroaches eat almost anything, from insects to breadcrumbs.▼

Silverfish are one of the most primitive insects. They live in warm, humid spots. Under the kitchen sink is a favorite place. ►

Spiders often weave silken webs on basement rafters. You can see little, white fuzzy balls where the spider makes its home. These are spider eggs. ▼

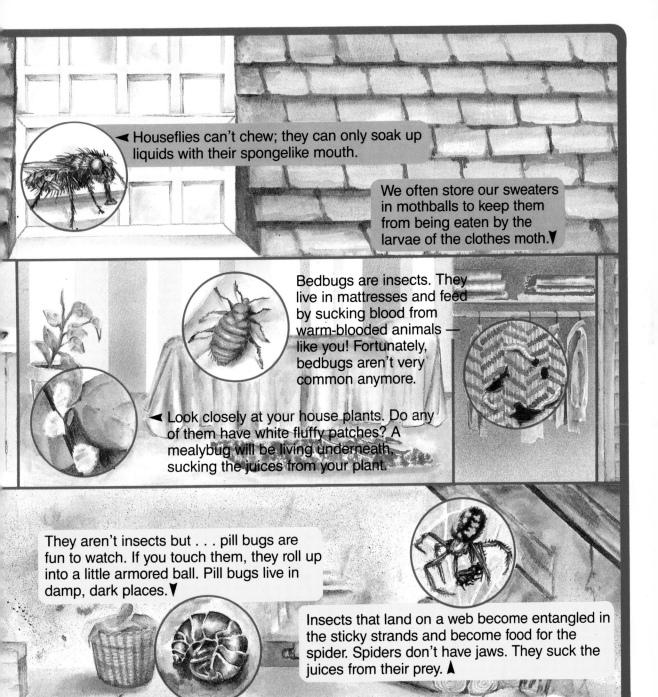

◄ Houseflies can't chew; they can only soak up liquids with their spongelike mouth.

We often store our sweaters in mothballs to keep them from being eaten by the larvae of the clothes moth.▼

Bedbugs are insects. They live in mattresses and feed by sucking blood from warm-blooded animals — like you! Fortunately, bedbugs aren't very common anymore.

◄ Look closely at your house plants. Do any of them have white fluffy patches? A mealybug will be living underneath, sucking the juices from your plant.

They aren't insects but . . . pill bugs are fun to watch. If you touch them, they roll up into a little armored ball. Pill bugs live in damp, dark places.▼

Insects that land on a web become entangled in the sticky strands and become food for the spider. Spiders don't have jaws. They suck the juices from their prey. ▲

LIFE IN THE FIELD

Insects that eat milkweed plants taste bitter to their predators. Their bright orange color warns predators that they taste terrible.

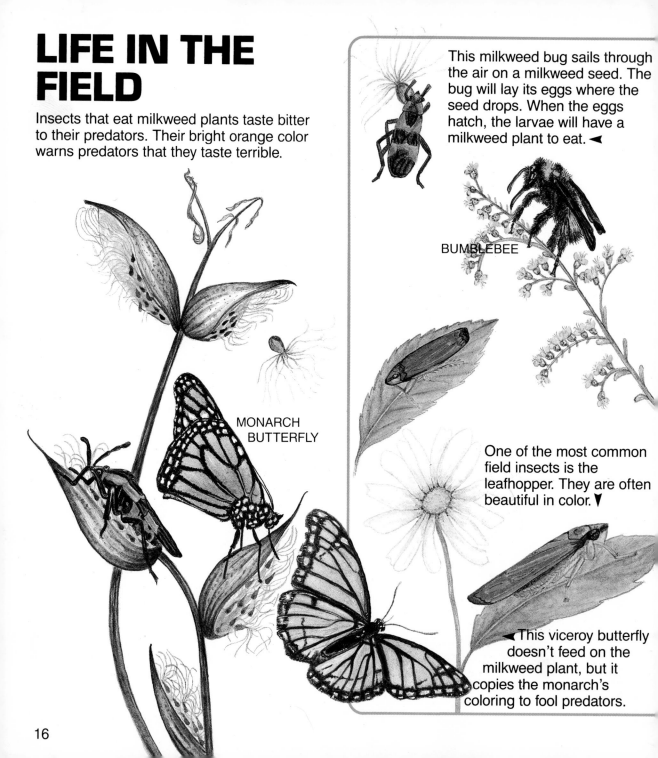

This milkweed bug sails through the air on a milkweed seed. The bug will lay its eggs where the seed drops. When the eggs hatch, the larvae will have a milkweed plant to eat. ◄

BUMBLEBEE

MONARCH BUTTERFLY

One of the most common field insects is the leafhopper. They are often beautiful in color. ▼

◄This viceroy butterfly doesn't feed on the milkweed plant, but it copies the monarch's coloring to fool predators.

THE GOLDENROD PLANT IS HOME TO SOME INTERESTING INSECTS

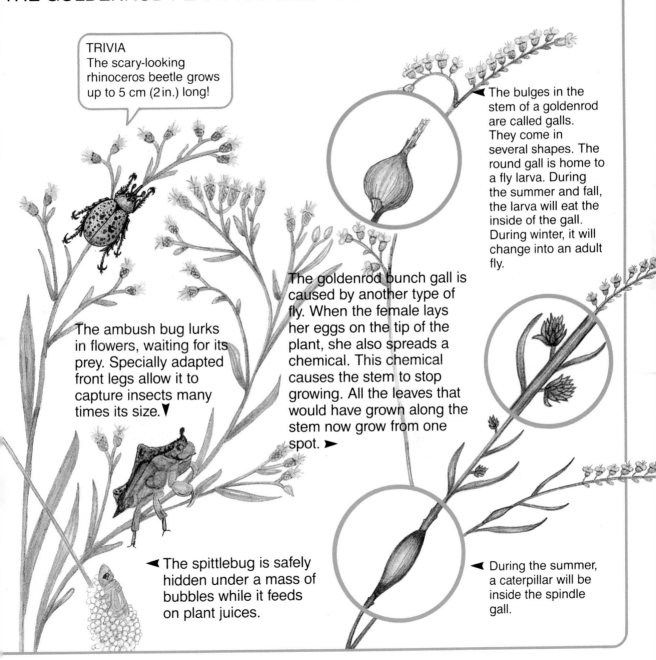

TRIVIA
The scary-looking rhinoceros beetle grows up to 5 cm (2 in.) long!

The bulges in the stem of a goldenrod are called galls. They come in several shapes. The round gall is home to a fly larva. During the summer and fall, the larva will eat the inside of the gall. During winter, it will change into an adult fly.

The ambush bug lurks in flowers, waiting for its prey. Specially adapted front legs allow it to capture insects many times its size. ▼

The goldenrod bunch gall is caused by another type of fly. When the female lays her eggs on the tip of the plant, she also spreads a chemical. This chemical causes the stem to stop growing. All the leaves that would have grown along the stem now grow from one spot. ➤

◄ The spittlebug is safely hidden under a mass of bubbles while it feeds on plant juices.

◄ During the summer, a caterpillar will be inside the spindle gall.

LIFE IN THE FOREST

Many of the insects in the forest, like the underwing moth, are well-hidden. Can you find where the underwing is hiding?

Tent caterpillars spin silken canopies to protect them from predators.▼

▼The white pine weevil may not be pretty, but it takes good care of its eggs. They are laid in the tip of a pine tree. When the eggs hatch, the larvae eat their way down through the tip.

◄A tree with white pine weevils is easy to spot; its tip looks like a shepherd's crook.

▲The aspen tortix caterpillar lives in a rolled-up leaf.

The biggest insect in the world is the African stick insect. It grows up to 33 cm (13 in.) long.

The pine tube moth caterpillar fastens pine needles into a tube and lines it with silk.▼

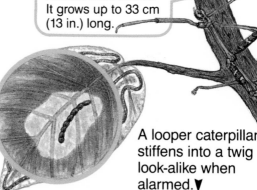

A looper caterpillar stiffens into a twig look-alike when alarmed.▼

▲A leaf miner has to be skinny! It lives hidden between the top and bottom layers of a leaf.

Even life under the bark isn't safe! Wookpeckers can hear a beetle crunching on the wood underneath.▼

LIFE BEHIND THE BARK

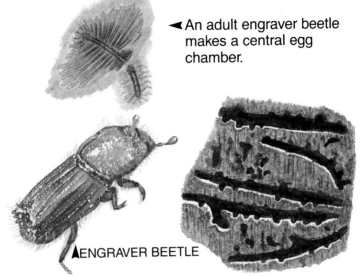

◄An adult engraver beetle makes a central egg chamber.

▲ENGRAVER BEETLE

When the eggs hatch, the larvae make tunnels like these as they eat between the bark and the wood.▲

▲Carpenter ants carve beautiful cities deep into dead wood. Unfortunately, they can't tell the difference between a dead tree in the forest and the lumber that is holding your house up.

LIFE AT NIGHT

Try a little night watching. During the day, spread some molasses or corn syrup on a post or tree. Return to the spot after dark with a flashlight. If you cover the flashlight with red tissue paper, it won't disturb the insects, and you can watch them at work.

HONEY

Fireflies aren't really flies at all; they're beetles. They flash at regular intervals to attract members of the opposite sex.

TRIVIA
In some countries, fireflies are so bright that people use them for flashlights.

INSECTS USE A VARIETY OF SENSES TO HELP THEM ESCAPE PREDATORS AND FIND MATES IN THE DARK.

Female moths release special scents to attract male moths. These scents are called pheromones.

FEMALE MOTH

TIGER MOTH

WHY ARE MOTHS ATTRACTED TO LIGHTS?

When moths fly at night, they steer in a straight line by watching the moon. When there is another light, the moths become confused and fly toward it.

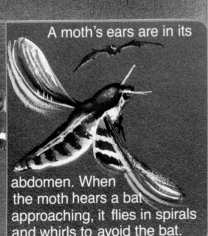

This bat won't hold on to the tiger moth for long. The moth releases a poison when attacked. Tiger moths also have special noisemakers to confuse bats.

Fireflies aren't on fire! The light is produced by a chemical reaction in their abdomen.

The large feathery antennae of the male cecropia moth enable it to detect the pheromones at a great distance.

A moth's ears are in its abdomen. When the moth hears a bat approaching, it flies in spirals and whirls to avoid the bat.

POND LIFE

TRIVIA
Dragonflies cruise along at about 40 kilometers an hour (25 mph), but they've been known to fly as fast as 70 kilometers (44 mph) an hour!

The giant waterbug injects a poison into its prey. This enables it to capture animals much larger than itself. The female has laid her eggs on the back of this male.

Dragonflies dart across a pond at great speeds, in search of food. A dragonfly's head is attached loosely to its thorax, and so it can turn its head in all directions. It has good eyesight and can spot its prey easily. When in flight, its legs fold up to form a basket shape, allowing it to scoop insects out of the air. Some lay their eggs as they fly over the surface of a pond.

Dragonfly nymphs are jet-propelled. They suck in water through their gills and then shoot it out. This way, they can dart quickly around the pond.

Young dragonflies can only breathe in water. Adults must breathe air or they will drown. When a nymph is about to change into an adult, it will climb a reed to shed its skin.

This strange-looking structure is the home of a caddis fly larva. Each type of caddis fly nymph makes a different home. Can you see another one in this picture?

Insects have many predators. Birds, especially, are an insect's enemy. Can you find the two insect predators in the pond?

Don't blame all the mosquitoes for those nasty bites! Only the females feed on our blood. The males suck plant juices.

The backswimmer spends its life swimming on its back. How are its hind legs adapted to life in the water?
▼

The water strider "skates" across the water looking for insects. It has tiny "snowshoes" on its feet to keep it from breaking through the water's surface.
▼

Mosquitoes lay their eggs in water. These eggs often form small "rafts" on the surface of a pond. When the eggs hatch, the mosquito larvae breathe through a "snorkel."

The water boatman looks like a right-side-up ▲ backswimmer. Both insects breathe the bubbles of air which get trapped beneath their wings.

The whirligig beetle ▲ never seems to know where it is going. It is well-suited to where it lives. It has two sets of eyes, one below the water and other above.

DRAGONFLY NYMPH

Young dragonflies, known as dragonfly nymphs, have huge appetites. They will eat many kinds of insects, including their own kind, and will even attack tadpoles and small fish.

23

INSECTS IN WINTER

Unlike mammals and birds, insects are cold-blooded. This means that their body temperature is the same as their surroundings. The colder it gets, the slower they move.

June beetle larvae move deep into the earth to escape the winter cold.

The egg case of a praying mantis is made of a hard foam that provides insulation against winter weather.

The poplar vagabond aphid's eggs are safe inside this gall on the leaf stalk of a poplar tree. These galls will stay on the tree long after the leaves have fallen.

The eggs of the oyster shell scale are hidden beneath the shell of the mother.

Mourning cloak butterflies hide in a sheltered spot.

Oak leaf skeletonizers spend the winter in cocoons spun along the veins of oak leaves.

Snowfleas (actually springtails) are often found hopping around on the snow in late winter.

Try looking through dead leaves in the winter. What insects can you find? If you're lucky, you may find hundreds of ladybird beetles hibernating.

MONARCH MIGRATION

A few insects migrate to escape winter. The most famous of these is the monarch butterfly. They fly up to 5,000 kilometers (3,105 miles) on their journey to Mexico each fall.

They will often congregate in huge flocks along the shores of Lake Erie and Lake Ontario. In mid-September, you can see trees covered in the orange and black butterflies.

Scientists place tags on monarchs' wings to help track this butterfly's migration. If you find a tagged butterfly, write down where you discovered it, your name and address, and mail it to the address on the tag.

Dragonflies move with the weather, too! In Europe, clouds of dragonflies fill the air during migration.

Summer afternoons are filled with insect sounds. Insects usually make noise by rubbing one part of their body against another. Insects use their music to attract mates. Most noisemakers are male.

Grasshoppers have 80-90 tiny teeth on the front part of their legs. Music is made by rubbing these against their wings. You can make a similar noise by rubbing your finger down the teeth of a comb.➤

Crickets have ears in their legs!▲

Crickets and katydids sing by rubbing their four wings together. The rough bottoms of their upper wings rub against a sharp ridge on the tops of their lower wings.▼

◄In some countries singing crickets are kept in cages like songbirds.

SEVENTEEN YEARS UNDERGROUND!

The larvae of the periodic cicada live underground, feeding on roots. After seventeen years, the larvae climb out of the ground. ➤

They will cover the trees, waiting to change into adults — if the birds don't get them first! Once their shells and wings have hardened, the male cicadas begin to sing. This helps them find a mate. After mating, the females lay their eggs in the bark of twigs. These eggs hatch into nymphs, fall to the ground and dig under the earth.

This cicada makes its music like no other creature in the world. Inside its abdomen is a drum. When the cicada flexes its muscles, the drum beats against the wall of its abdomen.

Other types of cicadas can be heard every summer. The hotter it gets, the louder they sing. Some people call them "heat bugs."

DRUM

TRIVIA
In the few weeks of its adult life, the male katydid plays its song 50 million times!

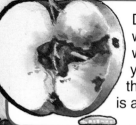

Did you ever get a wormy apple? Well, it wasn't a worm inside your apple, but probably the apple maggot, which is a fly larvae.

The larvae of the carrot weevil make tunnels as they eat through carrots and celery. (If you think the larvae are ugly, take a look at the adult!)

The tomato hornworm is beautiful, but it eats your tomato and pepper plants.

The lonely Japanese beetle eats almost everything in sight! Their big appetites won't leave much for you.

Earwigs don't do much harm. They eat only dead or dying plants.

28

GLY INSECTS IN YOUR GARDEN

The assassin bug is good to have in your garden. It eats other insects!

The larvae of the ladybird beetle may be ugly, but they help keep your garden looking good. These larvae eat a lot of aphides.

The praying mantis is a good insect. It is such a big insect-eater that some people even buy praying mantes to protect their gardens!

People used to be afraid of earwigs. They believed that earwigs would climb into their ears.

COLLECTING INSECTS

A magnifying glass will help you discover the amazing insect machine.

Nylons make good collecting nets.

1. Make a circle with a piece of wire, leaving ends 30 cm (12 in.) long.

2. Fold the open ends of the nylon over the wire and stitch it as shown.

3. Use strong tape to fasten the ends down to the sides of a stock.

4. When you capture an insect, twist the net to trap the insect inside.

Your collecting net will also work in water! Drag it along the bottom of a shallow pond. Turn the net out in a bucket of water. Now, inspect your catch!

A big sheet of white paper and a stick are all you need to collect insects from trees. Just place the paper on the ground below a tree. Knock the tree branches with a stick and watch what happens! Insects are easy to see against the white paper.

KEEP YOUR INSECTS IN JARS: Put 2 cm (1 in.) of soil in the bottom of the jar. Provide your insect with some food. A piece of the plant you found it on will do nicely. Replace the food when it becomes wilted. Keep the jar in a shady place.

Don't forget: Insects need air. Poke holes in the top of the jar or they will suffocate.

CAN YOU FIND THEM?

There are ten insects hidden in this picture.

(See page 32 for answers.)

In ancient Egypt, scarab beetles were sacred. The Japanese beetle is a type of scarab.

GLOSSARY

ABDOMEN:

The last part of an insect's body. The abdomen contains the stomach, heart and breathing organs.

ANTENNA:

A long slender feeler that sticks out of an insect's head.

CATERPILLAR:

The larva of a moth or butterfly.

COCOON:

The protective coating in which an insect spends its pupal stage.

COMPLETE METAMORPHOSIS:

The metamorphosis of an insect which has a pupal stage. Egg-larva-pupa-adult.

EXOSKELETON:

A stiff covering that supports and protects an insect's body.

GRUB:

The larva of a beetle.

INCOMPLETE METAMORPHOSIS:

The metamorphosis of an insect without a pupal stage. Egg-larva-adult.

LARVA:

The stage of an insect's life between hatching and becoming an adult or pupa.

MAGGOT:

The larva of a fly.

METAMORPHOSIS:

The transition of an insect from egg to adult.

POLLINATE:

The movement of pollen from the male part of a flower of the same type.

PUPA:

The stage during complete metamorphosis in which a larva changes into an adult. It is also called the pupal stage.

THORAX:

The part of an insect's body between the head and the abdomen. The legs and wings are placed on the thorax.

One is larva, pupa or antenna. Two or more are larvae, pupae, or antennae. One is metamorphosis and two or more are metamorphoses. Aphid is singular and aphides are plural. If you have more than one praying mantis, you have praying mantes.